10/28/16
writing on cover
notes

Ten Pets

The Sound of Short E

By Cynthia Amoroso

2

Can you count ten pets?

One pet likes to rest.

5

This pet is very wet.

This pet is in a tent.

9

A bell is a toy for this pet.

This pet is a gift for Ben.

This pet has
made a nest.

I think this pet
has met a pal.

17

This pet likes
to get a hug.

19

This last pet I like the best!

21

Word List:

bell	pet
Ben	pets
best	rest
get	ten
met	tent
nest	wet

Note to Parents and Educators

The books in this series are based on current research, which supports the idea that our brains are pattern-detectors rather than rules-appliers. This means children learn to read easier when they are taught the familiar spelling patterns found in English. As children encounter more complex words, they have greater success in figuring out these words by using the spelling patterns.

Throughout the series, the texts provide the reader with the opportunity to practice and apply knowledge of the sounds in natural language. The books introduce sounds using familiar onsets and *rimes*, or spelling patterns, for reinforcement.

For example, the word *cat* might be used to present the short "a" sound, with the letter *c* being the onset and "_at" being the rime. This approach provides practice and reinforcement of the short "a" sound, as there are many familiar words made with the "_at" rime.

The stories and accompanying photographs in this series are based on time-honored concepts in children's literature: well-written, engaging texts and colorful, high-quality photographs combine to produce books that children want to read again and again.

Dr. Peg Ballard
Minnesota State University, Mankato

Published by The Child's World®
1980 Lookout Drive • Mankato, MN 56003-1705
800-599-READ • www.childsworld.com

ACKNOWLEDGMENTS
The Child's World®: Mary Berendes, Publishing Director
The Design Lab: Design
Michael Miller: Editing

PHOTO CREDITS
© Bronwyn8/iStockphoto.com: 21; cynoclub/iStockphoto.
com: 9; Dave Bredeson/Dreamstime.com: 6; GlobalP/
iStockphoto.com: 17; odole/iStockphoto.com: 14;
onceawitkin/iStockphoto.com: 10; Serafima/iStockphoto.
com: 18; Studio Barcelona/Shutterstock.com: 5; sveta3/
iStockphoto.com: 13; Worldfoto/Dreamstime.com: cover, 2

ISBN 9781634070195
LCCN 2015930165

Printed in the United States of America
Mankato, MN
July, 2015
PA02267

ABOUT THE AUTHOR

Cynthia Amoroso holds undergraduate degrees in English and elementary education, and graduate degrees in curriculum and instruction as well as educational administration. She is currently an assistant superintendent in a suburban metropolitan school district. Cynthia's past roles include teacher, assistant principal, district reading coordinator, director of curriculum and instruction, and curriculum consultant. She has extensive experience in reading, literacy, curriculum development, professional development, and continuous improvement processes.